Eccentric Girl Press

ISBN 978-1-7385248-4-6

TRIGGER WARNINGS

This book contains mentions of bereavement, loss, ill health, disability, infertility, addiction, overdose, poverty, child loss, parenting, work issues, career change, inequality, dementia, homelessness, divorce, bullying, arranged marriage, relationship betrayal, perimenopause, prostitution, weight issues, anxiety, child marriage, rare disease, complex post-traumatic stress disorder, relocation, identity issues, neurodiversity, physical, emotional, financial and sexual abuse.

CONTENTS

Sam - Complex post-traumatic stress disorder, rare disease, anxiety

Elizabeth - bereavement, relocation, identity issues, overdose, addiction, poverty, neurodiversity, prostitution

Ruth – work issues

Jacqueline - stress, anxiety, work issues, perimenopause

Sarah - sexual violence, physical abuse

Becs – identity issues, parenting

Gina - addiction, weight issues, career change

Eden - mental health issues, bullying, complex post-traumatic stress disorder, domestic violence, homelessness, financial abuse, debt, divorce, loss, disability, neurodiversity

DEDICATION

For my dear friend, my warrior queen.
You inspire and encourage me, I value
the friendship and strength we share,
in the tough times and in the joy.
You showed me how to be proud of who I am

INTRODUCTION

When I went through trials in my life it didn't seem there was a way for me to genuinely connect with, or even hear from other people with similar struggles, who had gone through their issues to live a better life.

The times when I did meet women with obvious strength it was too intimidating to try and connect, I didn't want them to realise I wasn't like them. With the rise of the internet, it obviously became easier to meet your tribe.

In the years since I started writing and networking, I have been fortunate enough to meet some incredible women. With stories of pain, loss, fear, health scares, emotional, and physical abuse, challenge and ultimately triumph.

Women who looked those challenges in the face, rolled up their sleeves and created things that made better lives for themselves, and often a community for other people to step into.

These stories inspired me, and I began to understand they needed to be shared with other people, creating another way for people to connect with messages of surviving and thriving.

It was important to me I do something for others to help manage their worst fears, that they are the only ones having to struggle. That they are the only one life is 'punishing' or it's their fault.

That everyone else, particularly those they meet through work or professional situations 'have it all together'. They are somehow behind or failing at life. My own story started out much like that.

The women in these pages have generously shared their stories to help encourage and inspire other people on my website, and now in this book.

Being released on International Women's Day is no coincidence, it's a nod and a heartfelt high five to every woman who keeps going.

The other aim of the book is to raise money for, and awareness of, the two charities mentioned within these pages.

Educare Fund supports the education of girls at secondary school level, in Lesotho, South Africa, enabling them to have more choices in their lives.

And The Adjvir Singh Sandhu Leadership Foundation which works to create a world where motivated young people reach their full potential.

Through mentoring, and having the people to believe in, and support their dreams. “Our vision is of a world where motivated young people will reach their full potential as leaders”.

YVONNE

Yvonne began by saying that, like many of us, her life had not been free of anxiety or trauma, and she described it as a whirlwind. It was after she had her baby in 2012 this story begins, at that time, she was a driving instructor.

Yvonne explained she had always been small framed but after the baby she could not shift the weight. Many of you reading this might assume where the story is going, you will undoubtedly be wrong so read on.

Like a lot of women, she thought post baby weight gain was normal. It wasn't until eleven years later, while having dinner at a friend's house that she mentioned still trying to lose weight. She blamed herself for overeating in lockdown or thought maybe she had developed an intolerance or allergy.

At this point people who didn't know her assumed she was pregnant, even asking when she was due! Her friend reached out and touched Yvonne's stomach and said, "you need that checked out, that's rock hard, fat is soft".

Following her friend's advice Yvonne got an appointment with her GP, had some blood tests and waited. The results showed her tumour markers only one mark above normal, which didn't raise alarm bells, but the doctor decided to send her for a scan anyway.

The scan showed up a large mass on one of her ovaries.

What followed was months of tests and more scans before the team agreed to operate, as Covid was still around, this meant Yvonne having to isolate immediately.

The mass they removed (along with the fallopian tube) weighed 10kg (or 22 lbs) and was 38 cm (15 inches) long, she was incredibly lucky to be alive.

Unfortunately, instead of taking time to heal at home, she began to worry about money. Something many self-employed people will recognise, and she made the choice to go back to work just a few short weeks after surgery.

Yvonne was working every hour she could to try and catch up with her bills, which meant that she had stopped looking after herself again.

Eighteen months after the surgery, a fellow driving instructor who was aware of what she had been through, asked her if she would be interested in learning about becoming a personal and business protection advisor. Knowing what it was like not having any protection, she jumped at the chance to help other people.

Yvonne realised had she had the protection at the time of her surgery, she would have been able to rest and give herself time to properly recover.

The first step was to finally set up her own policies, so she would never be in that situation again. Then it was onto the training to become an insurance advisor so no-one else she met need suffer as she had.

Yvonne acknowledges she is shy, which is a refreshing change that makes her stand out in business environments – as she did to me. She told me of her hopes as her business grows, of overcoming this. And one day being able to mentor new people coming into the insurance business.

But shy does not mean lacking in confidence, Yvonne said "I know that I have the ability to be great at anything I put my mind to".

"Nothing easy is worthwhile, nothing worthwhile is easy. Hard work always pays off, creating the life I wanted has not been easy by any means, but it has been full of nice moments, and shedding a lot of old beliefs, fighting battles nobody knows about… not to mention the lack of sleep!"

CASSIE

Cassie and I met in the same pottery group, and although they were fabulous it was not her clay creations that made me take notice of her. It was her quiet humour and the odd quirky comment said in a super relaxed way that made me want to find out more… we got acquainted over several coffee dates, and as we began to share our stories, I knew hers needed to be shared.

It starts in a not unusual way, with being part of a quite turbulent family, but when as a still young child she lost her father, things became significantly worse. She was moved between relatives rather than staying with her mum, so she remembers this as a time not just of deep sadness and loss, but also of depression and disconnection from her mother and siblings.

Because of this Cassie grew up holding a lot of anxiety and negativity, which went with her into her adulthood. She told me about having battled an extreme lack of confidence, self worth, anxiety and lack of motivation.

In her mid twenties another loss of a close family

member led her into therapy, which she says "was the single best thing I could have done for myself".

Although it took years of sifting through, and deciphering everything from her childhood, to bring her to the mindset she has today, that investment in her wellbeing gave Cassie a whole new outlook.

Show me someone who experienced true adversity, and I will show you someone with something incredible to share.

While on her journey Cassie had endless jobs she found unsatisfying and unstimulating, experimenting with a host of different ideas, from baker to barista to driving instructor. The list would have continued on, but instead motherhood called, and she became a parent to two beautiful boys.

Cassie was adamant she was not at all artistic growing up, it was when she began experimenting with various artistic hobbies with her sons, that it set something off in her, it fed her new more motivated mindset, and she began to embrace creative outlets, like her pottery.

Three years ago Cassie decided on painting as a new hobby, and it became such a positive part of her life she didn't want to stop! So much so that the canvas wasn't satisfying enough and her love of creating wall murals began.

Over the weeks she showed me pictures of the characters as they took their place on the wall. Until the grand reveal of a Marvel city skyline with the Hulk, Spider Man Captain America and Iron Man.

The difference in confidence from that withdrawn child to now was obvious, here was someone owning their skill and talent. And she showed me the plans for a misty forest mountain project she had started in her living room (you can view a photograph of the Marvel wall on my website link in the resources list).

Sadly, for me at any rate Cassie and I don't go to the same pottery studio anymore, as she moved to an art class to hone her painting and drawing techniques. But I am so pleased she is prioritising something that is a deep passion for her.

Too many of us say 'I'll start later, when I have a less stressful job, or the children are older', all the while letting our talents go to waste.

Cassie hasn't got a clear plan for the future right now but says maybe one day her enthusiasm for murals may turn into a business, but for now she is focused on learning and practice.

That journey through anxiety, depression and therapy led her to make incredible art, and to a totally different mindset, she says "no two days are the same, if things don't go to plan that's okay. Take a breath, get some fresh air, and trust it will all work out".

NICKY

Nicky and I met on a public speaking course, she was the 'character' in our group, an eccentric, funny, intelligent woman. Who a little while into our acquaintance told us she was autistic.

I didn't understand much about autism then except what was portrayed in books and on television; and almost all these showed boys and men.

This was a whole four years before I found out about my own autism. And because one of my special interests has always been researching things, especially when it's about people and how they work, I made it my mission to learn about being 'on the spectrum'.

As I kept hearing it described in this way, I asked Nicky to tell me all about whether she considered autism her 'superpower'. She explained being 'on the spectrum' itself contained a huge level of diversity.

At one end you have individuals who appear to have 'nothing wrong' with them, and at the other end severely disabled people who need support in all areas of living, which didn't sound like any superpower I had heard of.

Because of this range it's something people don't necessarily understand, and when you don't understand something it's easy to come to the wrong conclusions.

Many people dislike the term 'high functioning' as it detracts from a person's struggles. It often just means they are more likely to be able to mask to blend in with their environment, but like a chameleon they are only changing their outsides to fit in. While the inside challenges remain exactly the same and go unnoticed.

Constantly having to adapt to the environment around them, so they blend in and not draw attention to themselves, is something a neurotypical person would not have to consider.

Nicky rightly pointed out that for the vast majority of autistic people it is the *environment* that is disabling, and terms like high functioning diminish the difficulties people face on a daily basis.

Noise sensitivity is a massive thing, she can hear electricity buzzing through cables, which makes her nauseous, and is extremely distracting. Vibration from things like excessive bass sounds from someone's car stereo can send her into sensory overload. If that overload isn't controlled it leads to a meltdown, and that's something every autistic person wants to avoid.

Nicky said these levels of anxiety, high levels of external pressures on how to behave in ways that feel, to them, unnatural, is what an autistic person experiences on a day to day basis.

As an autistic person your vocal and physical stims and habits are designed to help your brain stress relieve. But children who grow up being told to sit still, not fidget, be quiet 'and not be naughty' grow into adults with shame simply for being themselves.

They don't feel ok with the ways their brains need to regulate their emotional states which is as exhausting as it sounds.

Nicky told me that for her personally one of the most obvious effects of her autism is her hyper focus, which is an intense focus on a particular subject or task.

When in that zone everything else is put on hold, eating, going to the toilet, household chores, other jobs etc.... if somebody breaks her focus it causes real distress, essentially meaning she would have to start the task from the beginning to make her way back into the zone. She cannot simply turn her attention to whoever needs her in the moment, and then go back to what she was doing without a good deal of stress.

"I can focus on something so hard that I complete in a day what one person could take a week over, I get into a zone and if left to my own devices I am quite literally a machine. I can pick up on people's emotional changes, but I don't always understand my own emotions".

"My processing is delayed, so if I am reading a book, I will need to read the paragraphs several times to feel like the information has gone in, and it will take a day or two for it to trickle through".

Nicky admits emotionally she can seem distant, but this is also down to processing delays, if asked to answer a question on the spot she'll freeze. Not because she doesn't know the answer, but because her processing delays mean she needs a little time to consider the question and allow it to filter through.

"I am actually highly intelligent and given time and patience that intelligence will come through in abundance".

After the first shock of finding out she was autistic wore off Nicky found herself liberated, "having the label gave me a deeper understanding of who I am and how I had been hiding myself for my entire life. I wasn't weird, I was just wired differently".

"It explained why my life had been such a struggle and gave me a massive insight into how to cater to my strengths and balance my weaknesses. It gave me an opportunity to take my personal development to another level, to start to be myself, to stop masking who I am in order to fit in, with a society that disables me at every turn".

"It gave me the strength I needed to make a difference, not only to myself but for others too. To notice what masks I had unintentionally put on over the years, and to see why I had put those in place, it was, and still is pretty interesting to experience".

It explained why she had lived a life of addiction, Nicky realised she had been trying to give herself the confidence necessary to blend into social settings and numb her negative feelings about herself.

Her diagnosis gave her more compassion towards herself, and she realised when she is at her tolerance limit, she needs to remove herself from the situation, and that's ok, because that is what she needs.

Nicky went on to work with neurodiverse women, she strongly supports self diagnosis feeling that with the range of information and self testing available now it is perfectly valid. Being comfortable with her own diagnosis is a vital example others can draw strength from.

"You could ask a thousand autistic women what it's like, and whilst there will be similarities in the answers, all of the experiences will be different, that's diversity for you. For me it is both challenging and liberating".

She believes you can absolutely be autistic and not know it, whole generations (of mostly women) have been misdiagnosed with mental health conditions, or have slipped through the net. Often leading them to live troubled lives, filled with anxiety and depression, and very importantly, a sense of self built on an incorrect identity.

When you are able to function at a seemingly good or productive level, and all the difference is on the inside it is easy for autism to be missed.

So, was this ability to appear to fit in the superpower? it depends on which autistic person you ask. As Nicky said many times, the autistic individual isn't aware they are doing anything out of the ordinary, after all, how do you appreciate you are different when this is what you've always felt? how can you know everyone else isn't like this on the inside too?

KELLY

The first thing Kelly told me struck a chord, she had spent years in the corporate world, but never truly felt like she belonged there. She acknowledged being good at her job, working on managing major contracts, liaising with clients and problem solving. But deep down, she said "it never felt like 'me.' I often felt like I was working on someone else's dreams, not my own".

"I'd always been curious about human behaviour, especially having witnessed a loved one's struggle with their mental health. And often found myself wondering why I was able to stay relatively steady during difficult times, while others couldn't".

That curiosity never left Kelly and in 2015, she investigated training to be a therapist, but decided it wasn't quite the right fit. It wasn't just about understanding what held someone back, she wanted to help them reconnect with their dreams and turn them into something real".

So, she started a coaching diploma with The Coaching Academy.

As Kelly started her training, a new corporate role landed in her lap, it was challenging, engaging, and all-consuming, which meant coaching slowly drifted into the background. Even though she kept dipping in and out of the training over the years, she hadn't anticipated how much inner capacity it would require - especially when life had other plans, as it often does.

"One of those plans was the deep longing I held to become a mother, always imagining it would happen. but by forty I was still single, and had quietly started to grieve the possibility it wouldn't happen. Then in a beautiful twist, I met someone, we fell in love, we both wanted a family so began trying for a baby and, after a series of hopeful months and fertility tests, we prepared for IVF'.

"A month before we were due to start treatment, after what was just a small disagreement, my partner ended the relationship, saying he no longer envisaged a future with me. My vision of family - something I had held close for so long, vanished in an instant. The end of my own family dream was the deepest heartbreak I'd ever experienced".

In the aftermath Kelly clung to work to keep her going, but things were growing difficult there too after a change in management brought tension. Kelly found herself in a challenging dynamic at a time when she desperately needed peace, she requested mediation through her HR department, in the hopes of restoring calm, and on the surface things did smooth out. but the experience shifted something in Kelly, and she realised no amount of external achievement would make her feel seen.

That realisation marked the beginning of a deeper unravelling, and she started quietly planning her next move. But the universe wasn't prepared to wait, and seven months after her relationship breakup Kelly was made redundant. "I left the role utterly depleted mentally, emotionally, spiritually, and sank into a period of depression and anxiety, for a time I felt completely unanchored".

But in those difficult moments something shifted in her, and Kelly realised what she wanted was to create something meaningful of her own, rather than being at the mercy of circumstances. When she went back to coaching, it was with a renewed sense of purpose and energy. And Kelly not only finished the original diploma she had started, she also went on to complete an additional qualification.

As is usually the way, once someone works on the path they are supposed to be on, everything began to unfold. And Kelly's niche opened up to her – people in midlife navigating their own turning points, often loss, change, or a deep sense something no longer fit. Kelly listened to women asking the same questions she had once asked: "Who am I now? What comes next?"

Now with softness and purpose Kelly helps those in

midlife who have a sense of being stuck, invisible, irrelevant or at a crossroads, to reconnect with the essence of who they actually are, beneath the roles, the expectations, and the endless "shoulds".

Kelly supports people to uncover what they truly value, helping to build clarity and confidence and support them in designing aligned lives; fulfilling and deeply their own.

As if further proof of her passion was needed, since launching her business Kelly gained an ICF accreditation - the gold standard in coaching, held by only 4.5% of coaches in the UK. "With coaching being an unregulated industry, it was important to me to do this the right way - with integrity and a genuine commitment to transformation".

"My clients can trust our work together is not only powerful but professional and ethically grounded". Kelly acknowledges that like most of us, her story didn't unfold the way she thought it would. But says adversity has shaped her into someone who leads with her heart, and who can now truly walk alongside others as they find their way back to themselves".

At the moment the plan for the next few years include reaching more people and showing them a fresh start isn't tied to age, timing or what's already happened. It's never too late to become who you are, life doesn't have to be stuck, heavy, or like the best parts are behind you.

“I’d love to create a retreat at some point, a space for people to breathe, reconnect and simply be. Community is an important one too. During my own transitions, I saw how vital it is to have people who get it. I was lucky to have friends who showed up but not everyone does and it needs to change. I want to help build that kind of support for others”.

KATE

Kate's story is one I love because it's not about things going wrong or falling apart, it's about having the courage to rock the boat and follow your dreams. Not being afraid to stand out and doing something many people would consider crazy.

Although Kate says she had been planning her escape for six years, she went from a steady corporate creative career to being a self-employed artist. And yes, people did think she was nuts and/or having a midlife crisis.

She had been an interior designer and project manager for a global manufacturing company for seventeen years, when the company she worked for agreed a corporate sponsorship with Manchester United Football club. As part of this contract Kate was offered a six year secondment.

Taking it was a brave move because taking the role would lead to her job eventually becoming redundant. Which gave her the six years she needed to plan and build her own business for when her contract came to an end.

Since July 2024 Kate has been living her dream as a full time mural artist, including working in Australia. Although she says she is still new in the world of self employment she also describes it as “the best decision I ever made!” and not the midlife crisis her family feared! her plan in the short term is to “enjoy the ride and say ‘Yes’ to every opportunity I can”.

Although she feels lucky to come from a corporate background with marketing and sales experience, which did help her in the early days as a small business owner.

She did invest in some personal development with a business mentor, and found she knew a lot more than she realised, and Kate thinks you would too.

Having help gave her the confidence she needed to believe in herself to make her business thrive.

Kate's goal is to become a well-established and recognized mural artist within the south west of the UK. To be the ‘go-to’ that people talk about when murals are a topic of conversation, and I think she will be.

MONICA

We met at an art class some years ago, but only started talking when we realised we were both showing almost identical tiger paintings at the groups Christmas get together. We began by joking over whose painting was the best and ended up meeting for coffee.

At the time other than knowing her to be artistic I had no idea of the incredible force she actually was. Some people know her by her African first name Liphethiso, some by her second name Monica, but whatever you call her she is a truly inspirational person.

The story Monica told me about herself as a child says so much about the determined, norm challenging kind of person she would grow up to be.

"In primary school I played truant, doing everything I could to avoid school, from making my clothes dirty so whoever was getting me ready wouldn't send me, to feigning illness. Then I started taking myself to different schools in the area, joining any class that took my fancy!"

"Obviously, I couldn't follow any of the lessons, I never had any idea what the teachers were talking about. Fortunately, at some point I settled into school and began to enjoy it".

Even a spell in hospital as a child is described as serendipitous, as it led to her interest in the healthcare sector. "I was impressed with what those healthcare professionals did, despite my very young age I told everyone I was going to be a nurse or a doctor".

At the time Lesotho only had a few high schools, so anyone who wanted to continue their education had to be sent to boarding school, which is what happened to Monica. Her father although struggling as the only breadwinner, managed to pay her fees, but she was still in her first year, aged only thirteen, when her father died.

Family members knowing the school fees were beyond her mother's means suggested Monica take work as a nanny, something she had already done before starting high school. And for many girls that's what would have become their path.

However, Monica rebelled against this plan and told her mother she was going back into education and took herself back to school. Her intelligence and determination were noticed by the nuns who ran the school, and they worked to find enough sponsorship to cover Monica's entire high school years.

Without this help she could easily have not even

finished school, let alone go on to lead the life she did.

Using a local government scholarship scheme, Monica went onto university in Lesotho, where she finished her first degree in Botany and Zoology. Having no idea what to do with it apart from teaching, she started working at a couple of high schools but continued to look for a scholarship to study to be a doctor (or nurse).

Out of the blue Monica was offered the chance to study Veterinary Science in Canada, but she was told she had to decide in one week whether to leave Lesotho and everything behind and go.

Although worried about passing up the opportunity she felt there was no way to sort out everything that needed to be organised and leave for a foreign country within such a short space of time.

Monica was beginning to reconcile herself to the possibility of never getting an opportunity like that again, when she was offered a scholarship to study Pharmacy in the United Kingdom.

This time she had two weeks to make up her mind, apply to a university and leave Lesotho, and she did! She had a place at Belfast and went on to study Pharmacy, training as a practising pharmacist which she did happily until her retirement.

During her working years she became aware of the charity Action Aid, which helped poor children in

Africa access education. Seeing this as a chance to thank the people who had helped her, she chose to sponsor a girl.

In many African communities girls from poor families can be relegated to caring roles, often with no benefit to them, and perpetuating the poverty in these communities. Leaving women unempowered, with no resources, and no choices beyond raising children.

Monica told me she had always been concerned about the place of women in society in general but more specifically in poor developing countries. She understands the role of women in these societies and is aware of the unique contribution women make in their communities to bring about positive change. That's why for her, educating a woman has more impact than educating a man.

Unfortunately, unlike Monica's story there was no such happy ending for the girl Monica sponsored, not only because she didn't attend school, but because she was married off at fourteen.

Devastated Monica stopped donating to the charity and decided to look for a girl attending the Lesotho high school she had attended herself, to sponsor directly.

Now she says that at the time she had no long term plan other than to change at least one girl's life in the way her sponsors had done for her.

As she began to speak to friends and family about the girl, they were touched and wanted to do the same. Monica decided to set up Educare Fund, a charity to pay for girls education.

Gradually the number of girls supported annually increased, until by the end of 2023 sixty girls were being sponsored. Sixty lives changed, sixty young women's opportunities expanded due to the determination and spirit of one woman, who wanted to pay back the opportunities she had been given.

Monica's plan for the future is to secure the continuation of the work Educare Fund is doing well into the future, so she can eventually retire.

And she is always on the lookout for younger people with enough empathy and passion to carry Educare Fund's work into the future. To continue reaching many more girls from disadvantaged families.
"Kindness is a gift that keeps on giving, throughout my life, I received a lot of kindness, some from people I knew, and some from those I did not".

"Most without the expectation of getting anything in return. It taught me this is the best way to give. Give in this way, and hope those you give to, will give to someone else".

LESLEY

This woman goes by many names...Lesley, L M Krier, L M Kay, Carl Granger and Tottie Limejuice, these days most people call her Tottie or Tots.

“Words always came very easily to me, and I was always writing something, but not numbers - at all. I now realise I'm dyscalculic, but it was not recognised back then, instead I was told I was stupid or lazy, despite being neither".

That message is hard for a child to carry, especially when the label they are given doesn't feel right.

A lot of people are weighed down by negative messages they hear about themselves, but Tots didn't just rebel against being called stupid or lazy, she positively exploded it.

"My late father was a local newspaper editor, so our house was always full of books, many of which he had been given to review for various papers... I had my nose in a book most of the time, and when English author Alan Garner wrote The Weirdstone of Brisingamen, my father gave me the review copy and asked for my opinion".

At sixteen she sold a storyline for an episode of a popular 1960's television western. Although she can't say which one as she signed an all rights contract, she is allowed to say it was a prime-time series on the BBC but not Bonanza! so that might narrow it down. She was paid the princely sum of £200 (the equivalent of £2100 now).

"And while I would hate to tempt fate, I've always been able to sit down at the keyboard and bash out whatever was necessary. Just as well really, as I've been both a journalist and a freelance copywriter, both professions have crazy deadlines".

As a great believer in the power of dreams Tots story of how Ted Darling came to be, was one I loved. "This is going to sound incredibly cheesy, but I promise it's true! Most of the characters for my Ted Darling Crime Series came to me in a dream one Christmas some years ago. It was one of the most vivid dreams I can remember having".

"There was this detective, called Ted Darling, and he was telling me all about himself, his partner, his cats and his current case. There was so much detail, and amazingly I could still remember everything when I woke up, so having fed my dogs and put them out in the garden to play, I sat at my computer and wrote it all down".

"The first chapter went to a very blunt friend (she's from Yorkshire), and I was sure I would be given honest feedback. She said simply 'I want more', which is about as high praise as she gives. So, I kept on going, and going, and there are now twenty two books in the series”.

Tots’ major life change came about in 2007 with a move to France, which became the basis of her six volume travel memoir series, Sell the Pig by Tottie Limejuice (the origin of the name is explained in the books).

Despite the funny books the move came about from a serious situation, “when our mother developed vascular dementia my brother and I were not happy with the care available to her. Neither with carer's going into her house (disastrous) or later with residential care".

“We both lived too far away to monitor things, luckily at the time I was working as a freelance copywriter/copy editor, which I could do anywhere with an internet connection, so we decided to move to France together and bring mother with us”.

“I did need help getting her up and putting her to bed (due to some horse-related injuries I have collected over the years), but other than that I could take care of her, so I did. And she had four very good years, enjoying the sun and the lifestyle, before she died”.

Tots no nonsense attitude extends to the advice she shares “you can do it... whatever it is, you probably can *if* you believe in yourself. Okay, I will never 'get' numbers now, but if someone had helped me, and taught me to believe I could do it when I was younger, I could probably have been better at it.... and get a brutally honest friend to keep you grounded in reality".

"The funniest thing about my author career is always people's perceptions of what a crime writer should look like and their reactions when they meet me in the flesh for the first time. I make no secret of my age - I'm in my seventies - but fit as lop (which means very fit!)".

I do a lot of hill walking with my dog, always clocking up more than ten thousand steps a day. I'm always in trousers, usually with walking boots, so the silver hair is the only thing 'elderly' about me. And I still get people who assume I must be a man because I write crime!"

"My inspiration is Alan Garner because he was always so polite to me, a star-struck young fan. He once wrote me a letter to let me know of a programme on the radio in which he was taking part. He writes in the most beautiful calligraphy, so that's a much-treasured possession."

Tots said "Alan always remembered my name whenever he met me, and that impressed me. So, for that reason, as far as possible, I do always try hard to reply personally to anyone who contacts me".

Personally, she is starting to find she has itchy feet, as she has “mostly had rescue dogs, going away can be problematic, as they need a live in dog sitter with special experience, and that costs”. She has already decided that Rosie her current rescue will be her last, and in the future dogless days she will go off travelling.

She thinks France has excellent trains, as does much of Europe, and that it would be great fun to wake up in the morning and think 'I fancy a trip to Berlin today' and just be able to do it”.

KANAN

I was drawn to Kanan's calmness, and the something different about her, instinctively I knew I could learn from her. She became my coach, and an inspiration a long time before I knew we were in the same 'gang'!

"Once upon a time I was a shy, secretly reclusive introverted mum of two toddlers, the 'good show' I put on to fit in with the other mum's hid a bubbling mix of anxiety, self-doubt and physical exhaustion, because inside I knew I was different".

"Alongside this was fear for my kids, whose behaviour was challenging and often confounding, I suspected our son had ADHD. The lowest point for me, was seeing my husband having to sit on my son to brush his teeth, because he would simply not do it himself even after years of being "taught" this good habit".

After investigations and searching, Kanan's son was diagnosed with ADHD, and they later discovered this was actually autism, giftedness and ADHD, which Kanan and her partner call 2e or twice-exceptional.

"In going through this process with him we discovered – big reveal - both myself and my partner were 2e as well, and suddenly everything in my life, and my childhood finally made sense".

"I knew I needed to return to my yoga practise to help myself feel better, and it helped me rediscover the potential I had, that was hidden by my autism. I dove deep into everything I loved - personal development and spiritual growth. Invested in myself, and my desire to help others end their suffering".

Kanan went on to train as a yoga, mindfulness and meditation teacher and a life coach, from there she set up a service as a professional de-clutterer and organiser. She describes this as "following my passions and working hard to believe in myself, and what I was truly here to do in this lifetime".

All along Kanan says she felt inspired to make the big changes and choices in her life, due to a belief a happy fulfilling life is the birthright of all. Especially those misunderstood sensitive souls. She also carried an inner knowing she was here for more, to do more, to create positive change in the world.

And this is the part of Kanan's story that resonated most with me, and something I talk about often, everyone struggles with something, but if we focus, and allow those around us to focus, on what we *aren't* doing then we lose the chance to see, use and expand into all the amazing qualities we also have.

Whoever you are, and whatever is holding you back you will have things you can do, things you find easy, more than likely these things are your heart calling.

Now Kanan had found her dharma - to coach, mentor and help heal the wounds of other gifted and 2e neurodivergent people. To reach people who needed to know their diversity is part of the explanation for their challenges *and* their huge successes.

Transforming the lives, minds and hearts of gifted, ADHD, autistic and 2e adults allowed Kanan to feel grateful for the pain and challenges life had thrown at her. Which gave her the strength, resilience, inner peace and the courage she needed to offer this highly potent, deeply intimate shadow work.

The end result for her has been a transformation in herself and her family life, they are happy, healthy and well, and when bumps appear they are able to repair these ruptures.

She says her hope for the future is to create a community, which as an introvert, sensitive and autistic has always been a real challenge for her. After telling herself she didn't want or need it she now feels at a stage of life where she wants to share her energy and wisdom and receive this from like minded souls.

And now Kanan has a vision of where and how she is meant to bring this community together, to do something about this sense of being deeply misunderstood tackling this deep loneliness felt by many.

The sense of the world having so much surface level noise, when what we, as neurodivergent people want, and need is more depth, meaning and sacredness.

“I would like people to know and hold that you are perfect as you are. If you feel broken, know you are not. You may have emotional wounds that need healing, but you are perfect as you are. And you do belong, you just need to come back home to your true self".

"Use your body's wisdom - I say Feel It To Heal It; Name It To Tame It, manifestation of dreams is real, there are so many things I have created, including attracting some people into my world I would never have dreamed possible! Magic happens when we connect to our innate power.

NARI

I had the absolute privilege to meet with Nari to talk about why she, for me is an inspirational woman. She admitted when I asked her to take part she thought "why does she want to talk to me?" I think by the end of her story you will understand and feel the same as I do.

Nari is a go with the flow kind of person, one who sees challenges and just works through them, not a worrier by any stretch of the imagination. Although her upbringing was fairly strict, with the expectations of what she would do (and when) mapped out, she didn't really mind too much and followed the expectations her mother had for her.

When a match was found, she believed it would be a well thought out choice, and at twenty one she married Amrik. Nari smiled when I asked her how it had worked out so far, their thirty four years happily married shows their families definitely made a good choice.

It took some adjustment living with her new husband's family while he worked in London, but as she said that's just 'how things were'. She was very naive about babies, and when their son Ajvir arrived, she got told off by a nurse at one point for saying "it keeps crying". A sentiment I think most mothers will have shared at some point. Something steelier developed in Nari when she became a mother, she didn't want to set out their lives based on her expectations, or those of the older generations. Wanting them instead to have the freedom to explore what their hearts led them to. And as it happened this wish would become a guiding principle in Nari's future in a way no-one could have expected.

This desire for freedom and choice showed again when Ajvir was two years old, after trying to brush his top knot one last time, Nari decided enough was enough, and had his hair cut.

Not so dramatic you might think, but for a Sikh this was quite a thing to have done and caused painful ripples with his grandparents. But Nari was adamant if Ajvir chose to regrow his hair then it would be fine, but it would have to be his choice.

Time moved on, and their beautiful daughter Sabinder arrived, Nari describes her life as "perfect really", with a loving family, good husband, lovely home and two amazing children.

Ajvir took after Nari, not being a worrier and seeing the opportunities in life, he loved to try new things, including basketball and karate, and several other activities before a visitor from the Air Cadets did a talk at his school and that captured his imagination.

Children had to be thirteen to join, and although he had a couple of months to go before his thirteenth birthday Ajvir spoke to the visitor, and seeing something in him, she told him he could come along even though he wasn't quite old enough.

Rather than being another passing phase the Air Cadets became a passion, he wanted to be a fast jet pilot (think Top Gun), with him going twice a week after school, and often at weekends too.

When it became clear how serious he was, and finding it hard to get him to the group around work and home, Nari, who wanted to support him in every way she could, decided to leave work to concentrate on the family again.

With Nari and the family's support Ajvir rose through the ranks, in 2009 becoming the Lord Lieutenants Cadet for London, where he took part in Trooping The Colour, and met The Queen.

Being the boy he was, Ajvir managed to do this without causing issues with his school work, *and* while completing the Gold Duke of Edinburgh award, and meeting the Duke of Edinburgh.

Once he had set his mind to a goal Ajvir worked hard to achieve it, but it wasn't enough to succeed, like his mother he wanted to help others around him to achieve their dreams too.

A skill which led to his squadron winning the prestigious Lees Trophy, a prestigious award to celebrate outstanding performance and contributions within the RAF Air Cadets.

Something Nari and her husband did insist on, was Ajvir should go to university, they wanted him to have a fallback choice in case he wasn't able to have the career he dreamt of in the air force.

So, off he went to Durham university to study geology, staying an extra year to do a Masters, eventually leaving with a First class honours degree.

Finally, the time had come for Ajvir to pursue his childhood dream of being a fast jet fighter. The Ministry of Defence only chose ten pilots to become Fast Jet trained in 2015-2016, and you won't be surprised to hear Ajvir was one of the ten.

More dream experiences followed including flying with the Red Arrows, and MiGs with the Slovakian Airforce.

The understandable pride and joy of her son's achievements light up Nari's face as we are talking, but then she begins to talk about the next period of her life, which started with "the day my life went dark".

On 30th April 2016 whilst flying with a friend and colleague from the elite Linton-on-Ouse base Ajvir tragically lost his life.

There aren't words adequate enough to convey the magnitude of Nari and her family's loss.

We agreed the first year of bereavement goes in a flash, by the time arrangements have been made, a funeral has been held, and you have tried to find a way to breathe without the person.

As the anniversary came around Nari realised, she didn't want to do the traditional thing of spending the anniversary of Ajvir's death in prayer. Instead, she wanted *to do something* and decided to carry on his legacy with The Ajvir Singh Sandhu Leadership Foundation.

And with the same tenacity they shared with their son, Nari and Amrik launched the charity on his anniversary.

During our conversation Nari shared that after a few years she realised there was no answer to the endless Why? Nothing could help make sense of the death of any child, and especially not her incredible son.
The pain was, and is, a circle of ebbs and flows, sometimes less difficult, other times much worse. While the charity is an incredible thing to have created, she would, as anyone could understand swap it all to have her son with her.

Beyond the story of pain that led to its creation, The Ajvir Singh Sandhu Leadership Foundation touched my heart because of its ethos. The thread that runs from how Nari brought her own children up, through what they offer to the children the charity supports. Something that sadly, many children do not find in life - someone who believes in their dreams.

Through funding grants to providing mentorship, young people are encouraged to pursue their dreams, whether that be sporting or otherwise. As Nari said 'whether those dreams end up coming true or not, children need someone to believe in them'.

And that is why Nari is an inspirational person to me, a loving supportive mother, someone who has continued on despite the weight of unbearable pain, to create something which gives other children the chance to shine, just as Ajvir shone.

MORIAH JANE

Moriah Jane's main battles have revolved around her physical health, including short-term memory loss, borderline dyslexia, and chronic nausea which left her bedridden.

She told me it took twice as long for her to learn as her peers, as getting information from the short term to long term memory has always been a struggle for her.

And like many of us (me included) Moriah had to learn how her particular brain functioned to develop tricks for memorising new information. She admits her slow pace made her feel inferior to her peers, something else many of us can identify with.

The way others seemed to be able to pick up new ideas and memorise new words much faster than her was discouraging. She said "sometimes it felt like I would never catch up".

Alongside this, and although more slight than full blown Dyslexia (hence Borderline) hers certainly affects her writing. Letters tend to scramble across the page when she tries to read them, resulting in making spelling mistakes, or creating sentences that sound confusing.

Despite these challenges Moriah (like me, and many others) had dreamt of being an author ever since elementary school. Her issues meant finding work-arounds like needing to store notes for almost every small detail of her stories, where other authors can keep these 'on a mental file'.

She shared that "currently, I live in piles of sticky notes and journals to keep track of it all. But finding a way to keep track of information in a non-overwhelming way took a lot of time".

And the services that are supposed to support writers didn't always do the best job, her Dyslexia meant there were added areas in her manuscripts where an editor needed to give her advice on how to fix them. But the ones who had looked over her work insisted that the manuscript be perfect, before they started. That it was her job and hers alone to polish her manuscript into a flawless beauty.

This created a lot of stress for her, and as she now knows no fledgling author could work to that standard (and if we could no-one would need editors!), she was dealing with the wrong people.

Partway through college, she transferred to a different university to study Creative Writing as a major.

Before she could transfer, she needed to complete some core classes. Unfortunately the literature professor there hated Moriah. They thought the disability program was a sham designed to give certain individuals a free pass for their classes and so bullied any disabled students who attended the classes they taught.

It was only Moriah's closest friends who knew she was transferring to a college that was very hard to get into, and coveted by many students in the area. Being modest Moriah didn't want anyone to think she was bragging so kept the information to herself.

The professor also curated class schedules for each student for the next semester, recommending the hardest classes for the students they considered smartest, and those they disliked were recommended remedial style ones.

Moriah ignored the professor's antics, as she knew that she wouldn't be deciding any classes for her, regardless of whether she stayed or transferred.
And just nodded and pretended like she was considering the professor's choices.

Maybe because they didn't get a reaction the professor kept circling back to the 'lesser' students with recommendations, and asked Moriah if she wanted to take Children's Lit (claiming it would be easier than studying Jane Austen or C.S. Lewis).

After some back and forth Moriah said "I haven't decided what courses I'm taking next semester, because I'm transferring." The professor thought that Moriah was going to say she was moving to an 'easier' college, even suggesting the name of one.

When she said, "Nope. I'm going to The Master's University" the entire class broke out into a mixture of laughter and exclamations, everyone (other than the professor's favourites) congratulated her, asking about the new college.

I love this story so much, because someone with a modicum of power attempted to use that to belittle, and block the opportunities and creativity of a disabled person. BUT with grace and perseverance that person rose to the top leaving their bully behind them.

It was around this time that Moriah became aware that she could use her talents to support her faith.

Not wanting to read certain things, she developed the desire to write stories free of the content she felt convicted not to read. This gave her an all important goal to pursue.

About a year after college Moriah's writing had to go on hold for many months. She was bed-ridden most of the time, too tired and sick to sit at her laptop, and was eventually she was diagnosed with chronic nausea.

Although the following year she was able to restart her projects she told me that it was slow progress, with her poor health persisting for four more years.

How incredibly frustrating it was, how she had to pace herself, writing just a very few words every other day to help her make progress on her drafts.

What she said next really resonated with me and maybe will with you too, "it felt like a time where difficulties only stacked up and never lessened".

Her experience of trying to move forward with her diagnoses can, she said be "summed up in two words: stressful and discouraging".

Through this time Moriah's passion for crafting stories kept her going, even on the hardest days. They were an escape from her reality on her worst days and an exciting adventure on her best. She found solace in characters who struggled like she did, and watching these same characters overcome their difficulties was an inspiration and encouragement.
Moriah knew what they meant to her and wanted to create that for other people.

As we have already seen her writing journey was not an easy one, she describes it as "turbulent", and like us all went through many learning curves and still does.

She describes feeling "passed over" by many writing mentors, often getting told that they couldn't help her. Now she feels that some of these mentors simply didn't want to put the effort into a newbie, other's gave reasons like 'your writing is too advanced for me'.

This news was shocking but she found it incredibly encouraging, realising that these mentors were speaking from their own limitations.

However, it meant that she was thrown into the industry all on her own, suddenly everything was up to her, which felt exciting and scary.

She says that she has gained fantastic friendships along the way, although some days, she still feels like she has to do everything herself.

On other days, she receives the help she needs through irreplaceable author friends and supportive writing groups (which is where we met). It's a crazy rollercoaster ride of emotions some days, and a complete joy on others. Regardless it's a journey that has been worth it despite the circumstances and obstacles.

Moriah's journey has led to her becoming an independent author and publisher of three books (so far).

Originally, her plan was to start out as an indie author then go traditional. But the process for hold traditional publishing felt too crazy, needing an agent, querying, and needing stories to meet specific criteria for publishing houses.

She says "I am one of those authors who develops a vision for my story in my mind and simply cannot deviate, all the way down to the fonts used and cover design" Moriah needs the control so has stayed indie, and will continue to pursue an independent career.

Moriah describes the experience as amazing but also not what she expected, she thought that everything would change once she was published, that she would feel she had "made it" in the world, when in reality, not too much changed.

Writing continues to be challenging some days and a breeze on others, while some aspects of writing and publishing get easier, some never change. When she faces new obstacles she now reminds herself of past ones she has overcome.

"I think reaching these achievements is extra rewarding in the face of disabilities, life circumstances, or even health issues".

"It feels like having a super power almost! Just think of all the healthy, non-disabled individuals who say they want to, but still haven't even written a paragraph".

"But here we are, disabled, ill, suffering from the throws of life, yet we've popped out a book – or three". She says "publishing isn't easy, but if I can do it so can you, everyone's writing style looks different".

"Embrace that, uniqueness helps your work stand out and gives it a special flavour. Don't be afraid to experiment and pursue styles that work best for you".

Her hopes for the future include continuing to publish new and exciting stories, and to build a community of readers. She loves chatting about books, whether they're her own or someone else's.

And hopes to work on ways to manage her health so that she can start attending in person book events and selling her work at fairs, she describes this as an exciting but daunting task.

Beyond that Moriah hopes to find ways to encourage new and current authors to pursue or continue to pursue their dreams.

ANITA

Anita's story started many miles away physically, as well as emotionally from where she is today. Like many other women Anita's life was one thing in public, and something totally different in private.

We begin her story in Bulgaria where she earnt her Master's degree in Accounting and Auditing, going into a career as a Revenue Inspector for HMRC Bulgaria. Anita built a respected reputation within the industry, where she was known for her drive, a passion for numbers and her problem-solving abilities.

But behind the scenes of this professional success, her personal life was one of domestic, financial, and emotional abuse.

Despite her accomplishments, Anita felt trapped and powerless, stuck in a situation that went on for years. Like many women in domestic abuse situations, she wasn't in a strong enough place emotionally to just leave. Abusers have a way of keeping people stuck in place, no matter how much they may want to walk away.

Finally, the couple divorced, and although now away

from him, the stress of those years caught up with Anita. And serious health issues began to surface, which resulted in her being diagnosed with epilepsy and experiencing debilitating panic attacks. Both of which changed how she could live her life.

With her health and wellbeing reaching a breaking point, it became clear that rebuilding a life in Bulgaria was going to be impossible.

So, Anita made the bold decision to move to the UK for a fresh start, determined to create a better life for herself and her young daughter. Who, Anita said "inspires me to be resilient, to stay focused, and to never settle for less than we deserve".

"My journey isn't just about achieving professional success; it's about showing my daughter that with perseverance and belief in yourself, you can overcome any obstacle and create a life worth living".

Starting over was anything but easy, all the qualifications she had worked so hard for were not recognized in the UK. So, while managing her health issues she started studying to requalify, working for a cleaning company to financially support her family while she did so.

Any single parent who has balanced motherhood, work, and studies will know this was a serious feat. Anita says "this time was one of the toughest challenges I've faced, but it strengthened my resolve... and the values that have guided my personal journey—resilience, trust, and empowerment".

Slowly but surely, Anita rebuilt her health, amazingly overcoming both epilepsy and panic attacks as she found peace in her new environment.

"Looking back, I see how far I've come—from a place of uncertainty and struggle to leading an award-winning firm that makes a real difference for its clients.

"My story is proof that no matter how daunting the challenges, success is possible with perseverance and a commitment to your goals. This is the same hope and dedication I bring to every client I work with, helping them turn their dreams into reality with expert guidance and unwavering support".

Anita hopes that the work she does now will make a meaningful difference for entrepreneurs who, like herself, are determined to turn their vision into reality. "No matter how overwhelming the challenges you face may seem, you have the strength within you to rebuild and create something extraordinary".

"Life may test you with hardship, but those moments of adversity can also be the foundation for incredible growth and transformation".

TERESA

In 1999 Teresa was working as an executive secretary in one of London's prestigious utility companies and was trying to find a way to advance her career into management.

And that was proving difficult, not just because of the perception managers had of the secretarial role at the time, she admits she was also held back by her lack of confidence in her ability to speak effectively, not only at work but everywhere.

Teresa said that this allowed people "to control my future, my path, and my dreams all because I lacked the courage to stand up for myself".

Joining and walking through the door of a speakers' club for the first time was one of the hardest things she says she ever did – although it has turned out to be one of the most rewarding.

By the time I met Teresa she was a long way on from that shy, timid secretary who followed others. I met a strong, confident leader who people wanted to hear speak, and who people would listen to, when she did.

She credits having a mentor who had been through a similar experience and was willing to help her realise her potential as a powerful step in the right direction. Someone who not only believed in her abilities and potential, but "someone who wanted to help me unleash them and make them real".

In Teresa's case this just happened to be her existing boss, who took her under his wing and guided her through the pitfalls of promotion.

She said it took eighteen months of coaching, and a lot of hard work, going down many different, and sometimes very unexpected roads. Together they broke down the perception of Teresa's previous secretarial persona, built her confidence and self-belief to a new level, and gained her the acceptance of her peers.

Importantly they helped Teresa be heard, understood and remembered, and they have remained friends to this day.

Within a decade, she said she experienced huge personal growth, including promotions in her career, and taking the even bigger step of becoming the founding Director of her own consultancy, she says no-one would have imagined her being her own boss before.

The support that she had received made her passionate about doing the same for others through training and coaching. Teresa said "although it sounds cliched, the first step is the hardest, but as soon as you take it you will never look back".

And very fittingly she always recommends that people look for people who have already accomplished what you want to do, so that you can be inspired by them on your journey.

SAM

The first thing that struck me about Sam was her calm and peaceful demeanour, but when I got to speak to her properly, I realised that the peace she projected hadn't always been part of her life, and I liked her even more.

Starting in what she described as a stuck place, not least because of "a very long and torturous Civil Service career".

She developed Complex Post Traumatic Stress Disorder, and her son was born with Poland Syndrome, a rare condition (1 in 20,000 births) that is characterised by webbing of the fingers and underdevelopment of the chest muscles.

Her son inspired her to start a charity which she then ran on a voluntary basis, while still working in the civil service; Sam remembers this time as one of great disconnect.

So, what changed from disconnect to create peace? The moon! Sam started connecting with the moon in 2020 as a massive part of her spiritual growth.

Like many she believes in a strong connection to

the cycles of the Moon and uses those cycles to give her strength and power. “My resignation note to the Civil Service was written and sent on the full moon, which gave me strength”.

“Now, my business is all about peace and rest, I'm really driven and inspired by my need, want and desire to share my peace, and restful life, with people who exist in a world that doesn't give much space for these things”.

Sam is quite right when she says “This world invites us to do everything, except rest in many ways”.

Thanks to her spiritual development, and beliefs she describes herself as “no longer stuck, no longer small, no longer scared. No longer held back by the restrictions of either Complex PTSD, a horrible workplace, or the conditions that had been created in my mind as a result.

“I am free to dream, rest, meditate and create... I feel connected, restful, spiritual and authentic, in life and business”.

Like many people who have found themselves after great struggle, Sam wants to share her peace with as many people as possible around the world. To show people that there is so much power and creativity in rest, and peace within them, if they can just pause to look.

Sam’s big message to the world is that "whether you realise it or not, everything you need is already within you, you just need to be consistently quiet and listen. Start stripping away the layers that have held you back from that inner knowing, all you need to do is listen".

ELIZABETH

I met Elizabeth when we recorded a podcast discussion panel together, due to life and time zones, it took three months of near misses before we actually got to speak properly again. But as soon as we did, I felt the warmth of her energy, and I wanted to find out more about her.

This is her story, "for most of my life, the greatest obstacle I've had to overcome has been the belief that my worth was dependent on whether the people I loved could stay present, choose me fully, or remain emotionally available".

"I am an identical twin, and having my own identity didn't come until my adult years. My parents divorced when my sister, Becky, and I were two years old, and from that moment on stability was volatile".

"My mother, sister, and I moved in with my grandparents, who raised us with love and discipline. But also with the understanding that responsibilities came first, my grandfather was the man I looked to as a father, stern, loving, and dependable".

“He and my grandmother owned a janitorial business, and from around the age of five, my sister and I worked right alongside them, emptying trash, dusting, mopping, cleaning windows and bathrooms. We cleaned banks, churches, and office buildings multiple nights a week until we were fourteen, hard work replaced play most days and emotional needs were simply not discussed”.

“As my sister and I entered the sixth grade, my mom, sister and I moved out of our grandparent’s home to a new town that would offer us a better education. We lived in a small trailer with no insulation, and no central heating or air conditioning”.

“In the winter, we slept as close together as possible on a foldout futon cuddling to share body heat. In the summer, we would sleep as far as we could get away from each other to escape the suffocatingly humid heat”.

“Pipes burst, warm baths required us to sometimes boil water, washing our hair sometimes meant using a hose outside in the winter. I didn’t realise this was hardship at the time; I just learned to adapt and be grateful because it could always be worse”.

“In eighth grade I experienced the first moment when someone outside my family made me aware they didn't think I was enough. A boy I had considered a good friend, rode the bus with me one afternoon and learned that I lived in a trailer park, he told me we couldn't be friends anymore. That moment planted a seed of shame that stayed with me far longer than the friendship ever did".

"That belief, that I was somehow less, was quietly reinforced by an estranged relationship with my father, and later by the isolation I experienced at fourteen by moving from Louisiana to Pennsylvania".

"The culture shock was all-consuming, we had accents and had come from a tight-knit community, and suddenly we found ourselves surrounded by teenagers who made it clear we didn't belong".

"My high school years were painfully isolating, my mom worked two, sometimes, three, jobs to keep our bills paid. We lived in a neighbourhood where drugs, alcohol, and creepy older men were everywhere. I escaped with only a cigarette habit that lasted until my mid twenties, so for that I am grateful".

"In college, I finally came out of my shell and built lasting friendships, but in my romantic life I repeated what was familiar".

"Staying in a relationship that eroded my self-worth, until one night I discovered the man I was dating was prostituting women, when he asked me to meet another man behind a 7-Eleven so we could pay the rent".
"Staying with a person that could ask that of someone he "loved" was a dark wake up call of how bank-

rupt I was in self-love. And I immediately left the relationship and our apartment, moved home, and started over".

"While I tried to figure life out, my sister had graduated from college, was expecting a baby, and had moved to Virginia for a great job opportunity. The birth of my nephew changed everything, he helped my sister and I grow up; just by arriving he made us better people, and I have immense pride in being his aunt, his existence gave me a purpose".

Then Elizabeth met Neil.

"When we first met, I was unaware he was recovering from an alcohol and drug addiction; but he was sober the entire time we were together, until the very end".

"We made each other better people, and for the first time in my life, I felt deeply chosen. He became my anchor, so when after five years together he proposed on September 8, 2013 (when he was thirty two and I was twenty nine), I said yes without an ounce of hesitation".

"I was so excited about my future with him, unfortunately eight days after our engagement, my grandfather passed away. I held his hand as he took his last breath".

"Then, just ten days later, Neil relapsed and died from an overdose while at his nursing job; the grief was sudden, violent, and disorienting".

“Losing the two men who represented safety and love within ten days of each other forced me (eventually) to confront a lifelong pattern; I kept attaching my sense of worth to people who could not stay”.

“After losing my grandfather and Neil I didn’t make good choices, I survived by creating more versions of ‘joy’ that numbed the pain instead of healing it. I kept going, but I wasn’t really living”.

“Eventually, I found myself in a personal spiralling hell. For a long time, struggle wasn’t just a feeling, it became who I believed I was – I was the girl that lost them, so *I* was lost, ‘lost’ was my identity and that was heartbreaking”.

“The mornings were the hardest, I would wake up and immediately check in with myself hoping and begging that none of it was real. "*Please God, let this be a nightmare*". But reality always came rushing in, crushing my chest and tightly gripping my heart. I didn’t even want to open my eyes”.

“Extreme grief, deep sadness, and an overwhelming inability to breathe, settled into my chest and made a home there for months upon months. I had to talk myself through every single step of the day”.

Elizabeth would have to face the reality every day that it wasn’t a dream, “he’s gone, they’re gone”, and she would tell herself “one day this will make sense in a way you can’t see today, open your eyes, sit up. Put your feet on the floor, walk to the bathroom, turn on the water, undress, take a shower."

"Every day required that same agonizing process, one unbearable step at a time. It was hopeless, heavy, dark, my world halted while everyone around me got to keep on living. I didn't know if I would ever genuinely smile again, and if I'm being honest, I didn't want to".

"When I revisit that time in my life, I can still feel the weight of it in my body, that tells me it still lives in me. Once you've known that depth of loss, it's far too easy to return to that place".

"I don't believe grief is something we ever fully recover from, but I *do* believe we can choose what we want for ourselves, and I love that we can decide what happens next".

"Four years after losing Neil, I met my husband Chris, Chris is my best friend and greatest love. He accepted every part of me, even the empty parts left behind by Neil".

"He has given me a beautiful life, and we have two wonderful boys together, Beckett and Bronson. Chris is a private person and also in recovery, he has been sober for five years, and like many, his journey has included struggles that showed up differently over time. Emotional expression does not come easily for Chris, and there are times when distance shows up".

"This has asked us to confront and heal places of

mistrust in our marriage. Navigating that nearly unravelled me, because it activated the same sense of worthlessness and the not enough-ness I thought I had overcome. But we continue choosing each other through honesty, connection, repair, and growth".

"I made a choice not to abandon myself, gave him grace, and, as a couple, we choose to face things together. We communicate, we slow dance almost every night, plan for our future intentionally. Parent two very different little boys (our oldest is autistic), and we have had to be creative about keeping our relationship front and centre".

"Overcoming heartbreak, loss, and addiction was part of changing my belief that my worth is determined by whether or not someone else can show up fully".

"Oddly, when I was in tough times, I didn't always recognize that I was struggling, so sometimes it was bliss... as ignorance is! I didn't feel struggle until my losses forced me to see it".

"After everything I had lived through - loss, grief, survival, endurance - I could no longer pretend that a life built around productivity, performance, and checking boxes was enough. Corporate accounting gave me stability, structure, and safety, but it did not give me meaning or purpose. And after grief, feeling alive and being purpose-driven became non-negotiable for me".

“Life was stripped down to its most essential truths, it showed me how quickly everything can change, how fragile time really is and how little the things we chase for security matter when love is gone”.

“Much of my life had been spent surviving and doing what was practical, responsible, and expected of me. However, survival wasn’t and isn't enough, we waste so much time worrying about things that don’t matter in life’s big picture”.

“Grief taught me how heavy life becomes when joy is absent. It also taught me how intentional joy must be when it has been lost. Once I knew what it felt like to wake up each day not wanting to open my eyes, to move through life one agonizing step at a time. I learned what it took to slowly come back to myself, to choose to stay, to soften again, and to allow deep, nurturing connection in”.

“It also made me realize how deeply skilled I am at connection, and I began to see that the qualities developed through loss - emotional attunement, deep empathy, the ability to sit with discomfort, and the courage to rebuild - were not accidental”.

“I could see how many women around me were functioning, achieving, and holding everything together, while quietly feeling numb, depleted, and disconnected from themselves. I recognized them because I recognized the old version of me”.

“Leaving my corporate accounting career wasn’t

reckless, it was impossible to separate who I was becoming from how I spent my days. I felt called to create space for women to reclaim joy".

"Towards the end of my accounting career, it became harder and harder to hide what I was thinking. I could feel myself rolling my eyes so loud sometimes in meetings that I was sure they were going to ask me to leave before I was ready to give my resignation".

"For me, joy is not the absence of pain, but the presence of self, and the knowing that we only get one life (as far as we know) to enjoy while we are here!"

"As I went through my coaching program I struggled to put a label on the kind of coach I wanted to be, until my own coach stopped me as I rambled on about what I could call myself, and said

"Elizabeth, you are a Joy Coach, when I think of you, I think of joy." I laughed at him, and thought, who on Earth needs a Joy Coach?"

"So, I tried on every title that sounded good to me, and after I was certified began coaching everyone that would say yes! I was a relationship coach, a teen coach, a mindset coach, a confidence coach".

"Despite hearing it and knowing deep down that I am 'joy', it took me almost two years to get comfortable with calling myself a Joy Coach, and even now, I sometimes pepper in something else, "Joy AND xyz Coach".

"Becoming a joy coach was my way of choosing life, transforming grief, a lost sense of 'I am', and self-love bankruptcy into purpose. I get to honour everything I've lost by helping other women remember who they are beneath their responsibilities and roles".

Elizabeth told me that she hopes her work continues to be a bridge for women to go from feelings of numbness to utter aliveness. "I want to help women remember that even after heartbreak, even after disappointment, even after years of putting themselves last, joy is still there".

"In the coming years, I hope to speak more and tell the truth about loss, love, healing, and choosing yourself again and again. To create spaces where women feel seen, understood, and brave enough to imagine a life that is good on the inside, not just one that looks good from the outside".

"Now I am fully submerged in a life that feels 'so me', one where my days reflect what matters most to me, and my work comes from the deepest parts of who I am. Reconnecting women with the parts of themselves they've lost amongst responsibility, grief, motherhood, marriage, expectations, and doing the right thing".

RUTH

In 2018 I went to my first ever business networking meeting as an author, little did I know that in that room was someone who would become not only a supporter of my journey, but a true inspiration to me.

Her warm welcome and friendliness throughout the lunch wasn't just a front to bring me in or sell me anything. Ruth just wanted to really find out where I was at, and how she could help. With the writer's life generally being quite a solitary one, this connection was really needed.

Even though I left face to face meetings just before the pandemic Ruth continued to be a support to me whenever I called on her for advice, and this has included advising me on the best meeting rooms, to telling me the best place to buy chicken soup when I had a five week chest infection... and yes it did help!

This says a lot about the quality of the lady, Ruth describes herself as warm, helpful and kind, and I have never met anyone who would disagree with that.

And this goes to the heart of what makes Ruth inspirational to me, because it is easy to get caught up in our own lives, to not be the best people that we can, just because helping people is the right thing.

By embodying this fantastic quality Ruth motivates me to try to be a better person in both my business and personal lives.

And I know this effect hasn't just been felt by me, Ruth said the thing she loves most about her network is that "members are genuinely interested in each other, that they also work on *how* they can help each other. Which is always more than just buying people's goods and services".

Ruth is a graceful swan, always helping, always kind, always present whatever is going on for her network, her friends and family. She is very much the kind of woman I aspire to be.

Ruth describes her groups as tight knit, without being cliquey, with a real family atmosphere, and having visited many of the groups within the network I would agree. And it's her fifteen years getting to know people that give her an extraordinary bank of knowledge, and veritable army of people to call on.

I love Ruth's wisdom, and her mantra (if she had one) would be "if you promise something do it, and be respectful, always".

JACQUELINE

The way this person came into my life proves to me that you never know the effect that you are having on someone else without even speaking to them!

Our non-meeting happened at a business thing, where I missed out on speaking to her when I had to leave before the lunch and mingling started.

However, her infectious laugh rang through the room, and meant that she stuck in my mind, so when I was thinking about finding someone to upgrade my non-existent fitness regime, she was the first person I thought of.

As we got to know each other, I got to see not just what a ball of energy she was, but that she had a real understanding of stress and anxiety, and how this can hold you back from achieving your fitness and wellness goals.

This kind of genuine understanding often comes from someone's struggles, and Jacqueline explained that stress and anxiety had been a major factor in leaving her earlier role in Senior Management with the Drug and alcohol service.

For me when someone you admire who seems to have everything under control shares their own struggles, I get a boost, if it can happen to them, then I must be more ok than I thought. It reminds me that you never know what someone else is going through until you really connect, and that there is bound to be someone 'out there' thinking that you are the person who has it all together.

It wasn't until later when doing a Menopause and fitness first aid training course that she realised that her stress and anxiety issues, and plummeting confidence around that time was related to the perimenopause. And a passion for connecting women, who were going through similar issues through their menopause journey was born.

Jackie didn't want other women to feel alone and knew that getting their questions answered about the transition they were going through would help. That the right information about nutrition, mindset and movement would make a massive difference to people.

This connecting of women started not long after, while at a local women's meeting members were encouraged to write their goals for the coming year, and when Jackie read hers aloud – to bring a Menopause Café to the local area, a local reflexologist, had thought of the same idea so they joined forces to get the project started.

During lockdown the café had to go on hold, but as things re-opened Jackie was approached by the Chair of Waltham Forest Women's Network. This is a community-based organisation started in 2005, by a group of local women enthusiastic about empowering local women through bringing them together.

They wanted to know when Jackie planned to re-start the Menopause café, WFWN loved the idea so much, and it fitted so perfectly with their vision to empower and connect women to each other to support them to lead healthy and happy lives, that they asked Jackie to become a committee member, that they relaunched the café as a collaboration.

In 2022 Waltham Forest Women's Network won the Waltham Forest for All award at the Pride of Waltham Forest Awards. It was such an honour as this event is to acknowledge and thank the people in the community who go above and beyond.

Whether they're the quiet heroes or the stars of their local neighbourhood, they are open to all groups whose projects or activities have worked across multiple faith, or community groups to bring these groups closer together.

Since that initial collaboration Jackie has become the Chair of WFWN, and as always, she has big plans for the future. Which include continuing to connect women within the borough through different activities. Continuing with her Menopause & Women's health café, and expanding out to include different women's health issues that need further support.

She is also building a new project which includes nutrition, mindset, menopause, and movement on a membership site, so that she can reach women worldwide to make sure they have access to the information they need about this important part of their lives.

Moving from her own difficult perimenopause journey, to becoming a guide and support for other women, to being the chair of an award winning local organisation, no wonder Jacqueline's energy and laughter can shine across a room.

SARAH

Seeing Sarah at a ladies lunch I was instantly drawn to her energy, passion and honesty, she looked like a million dollars and then some. She owned the room without being over the top, not an easy thing to pull off.

So, of course I instantly wanted to be abit like her, while being a tiny bit intimidated to approach her. I need not have worried, she was absolutely lovely and joy of joys happy to stay in touch.

Since then, I have learnt about her incredible interactive theatre company, which was formed out of a desire to address inequality in society. Their message being a fearless one of making theatre to challenge hate and prejudice, combat discrimination and create equality and inclusion.

Their plays tackle the 'scary' topics in society: homophobia, racism, domestic abuse, county lines, racism, consent, sexual health, bullying and healthy relationships.

Things that didn't used to be spoken about at all, that thankfully are very much part of the conversation now.

Although we all still need more education, and Sarah helps people to understand the big issues so they can support and empathise with others to create the changes that make the world better for everyone.

Many people would agree with this, but not many people would be prepared to stand up and make this their lives mission. So how did this happen?

Sarah explained that she had always wanted to be an actor and got into top drama school Rose Bruford, which specialised in using theatre to make change.

However, at the age of eighteen she was in a physically and mentally abusive relationship with a man, who, when she finally found the strength to leave him, raped her. "I had so many feelings and so much grief from what had happened that I didn't tell anyone for years".

After getting her degree in Community Theatre Sarah went on to qualify as a drama teacher, worked for a TIE company, and started a youth theatre.

She realised that this specialist form of theatre could be used to explore healthy relationships with young people, and that would help reduce the amount of young people going through similar situations to the one she found herself in as a teen.

With that in mind she started her own theatre company Theatre Inspiring Change, Sarah said "I guess you could say that I found my voice at TIC Box Productions".

And it's that voice that has been creating positive change ever since. Being nominated for, and winning awards left right and centre!

In 2019 they won Community Champion at the Best Business Women's Awards. TIC was shortlisted for a European Diversity Award, nominated for a National Diversity Award *and* were nominated for a gender diversity award.

In 2020 after a successful national tour to young people of 'The Bruise You Can't See', TIC were finalists at the National Diversity Awards. And Sarah was the winner of Silver Most Inspiring Businesswoman, at Best Business Woman Awards.

It didn't end there, 2022 saw them win the Shining Star Award, with Sarah Silver Winner as Most Inspiring Businesswoman of the Year at the Best Business Women Awards. And Theatre Inspiring Change were shortlisted for a European Diversity Award.

And just as important to Sarah as all the public recognition, is having reached over 88,000 young people and adults, with TIC performances. She feels they have made a genuine difference in all these lives, engaging with everyone, no matter their location, financial status, or age, by promoting gender diversity and equality.

"You can use whatever you have been through to help others, in my case with our plays combatting hate and inspiring equality. I am proud to speak from a place of authenticity, and power having come out of the other end and turned my life around".

BECS

"Looking back, I was fiercely independent, career-driven, and competitive, but I was also disillusioned by the corporate world".

"I had bought into the narrative that success was linear: by thirty, you climbed the ladder, ticked off milestones, and followed a set path defined by societal expectations. I didn't realise then that I could create my own version of success—that I could carve a path that truly felt like mine".

"Children weren't in my plan, so, when I unexpectedly became pregnant with my eldest daughter, it was a shock. I couldn't reconcile the idea of having children with my definition of success. I didn't believe we, as women, could have it all - it was one or the other".

"Returning to work after maternity leave was a pivotal moment, on paper, my employer did everything right, I had HR discussions, Keeping in Touch days, and I was genuinely looking forward to getting back to work".

"I will never forget the excitement of trading in my

huge nappy bag for my small work handbag and dancing down the train station platform".

"But after a few weeks, something still felt off, I was existing, not living, and I didn't recognise myself in the mirror".

"At work, I showed up differently. I made decisions I wouldn't have made before. I felt confused, and that confusion spilled over into my relationships. What I eventually realised was that I had changed".

"Having a child was a profound, life-altering experience that shifted how I saw the world and how I wanted to show up in it".

"But like so many mums, I hadn't processed that change, time was scarce, and I was putting everyone else's needs ahead of my own. My return to work felt like a cold, hard smack in the face, highlighting that I couldn't show up as I had before, not because I wasn't capable - I was more than capable - but because my beliefs and priorities had evolved".

"I've learned that we *can* have it all, but "all" isn't a one-size-fits-all concept. My definition of 'all' used to be handed to me by society. I needed to take the time to redefine what it meant for me, and finally I was able to create a life that aligned with my values, my ambitions, and my whole self".

Your 'all' and mine may be completely different, and that's perfectly okay. The beauty lies in discovering what it means for you".

"Fast forward to now: I have two beautiful children, I've been promoted to a Head of Department role, and I've built a coaching business that helps other women navigate this complex, transformative journey".

"Through my work, I focus on the deeper, often-overlooked aspects of returning to work. It's not just about childcare logistics or HR policies - it's about empowering women to process their changes. Embrace their evolution, and make choices that feel right for them".

"Women simply don't get the support they need to transition into parenthood and then back to their careers - and that support is so desperately needed. There are programs to help women return to work, but they often focus solely on logistics. While those are valuable, they only scratch the surface".

"I work with a lot of ambitious, career-focused women who already excel at handling logistics. They might need some guidance navigating difficult conversations, but they certainly don't need to be shown how to schedule childcare!"

"Yet, many of them still feel 'chaotic' and struggle to recognise who they are or what they could be doing. What they truly need is something deeper - support that acknowledges the personal transformation they've undergone".

"In my view, this is the part of the conversation

that's missing. The Transition. Becoming a parent is a profound, life-altering event, and it changes how we see ourselves and the world. These shifts leave many women feeling different from who they were before".

"When they return to work, they expect to pick up right where they left off, but it doesn't feel right when they do. They can't pinpoint what it is, and that leads to self-doubt, and questioning everything from their decisions to their identity".

"My clients often describe this state: juggling exhaustion, navigating careers, and discovering a new version of themselves. They feel pulled in every direction, worry they're failing, and sometimes struggle in their relationships. Add in hormonal changes and the pressure of "getting it all right, and it's no wonder so many women feel stuck in survival mode".

"This experience is far too common. When you're exhausted from lack of sleep, navigating a career, and discovering a new version of yourself, having external support can be game-changing".

"Statistics show that 85% of women leave the workforce or reduce their hours within the first four years of returning to work after having their first child. That's an insane loss of talent!"

"The real issue lies in how we approach the return to work. it's about truly understanding the individual.

We need to recognise the transition they've undergone, explore how their values align with their workplace, and foster a sense of belonging".

"Many return-to-work plans assume that women come back with the same skills, mindset, and outlook they had before. But what if we flipped that narrative? What if we assumed they came back with more? more resilience, skills, perspective, leadership and drive?"

"By focusing on the person and rebuilding that connection, we could harness their full potential and create incredible possibilities for individuals and organisations alike".

"For the pragmatists, it's simple: a diverse workforce is a stronger, healthier one, and women are a crucial part of that. Supporting women to return to work is not just the right thing to do - it's a strategic advantage".

"At the heart of it, I believe that everyone deserves to win at work. Right now, some groups face more barriers than others, and that's something we need to address".

"By providing equitable support, we can create workplaces where everyone feels they belong and has the opportunity to thrive. I want to change those outdated ideas about what it means to be a successful career-driven woman *and* a parent".

"I am excited to build a space where women can

come together, share their experiences, and empower one another. It's about connecting with people who truly understand what you're going through, lifting one another up and learning from each other. Finding my own tribe was a turning point in my journey, and now I'm passionate about helping others find theirs".

"When women unite and invest in these connections, we become a force for change. Together, we can shift workplace cultures, challenge outdated norms, and create environments where everyone feels they belong".

"I don't love the word 'balance' because it suggests we need to keep everything in a constant, equal state - and let's face it, that's just not realistic. Instead, I prefer to aim for harmony or synchronisation".
"These words better recognise the give-and-take that is required to juggle all the things
in our life".

"This perspective also helps us let go of guilt when one area of our life takes priority over another on a given day, because the tables will flip the other way at some point! It gives us the permission to do one thing over another and ensures we are kinder to ourselves".

"By helping women reconnect with themselves, we can redefine the rules of what being a parent and a professional looks like".

GINA

There was a lady with the broadest smile who popped up on my social media feed from time to time, her posts always connected with me, either because they were funny, or because they were really touching.

One day her post shared a more personal side to her story not only was I honoured to be part of her audience, and knew she was the kind of person I needed in my tribe.

“I am so enthusiastic about sharing my story, because I truly believe that we are NEVER too old, and it is NEVER too late to step into the best version of yourself and be authentically you”.

“Before I was fat, frumpy, drinking way too much, with low self-esteem, and no confidence. I was depressed and generally feeling unloved and invisible”.

“I can pinpoint the thing that inspired me to make big changes in my life, acknowledging, accepting and then taking action to deal with the thirty eight year long drinking habit I had accumulated".

"That was the hardest, and best thing I have ever

done in my life, with professional help I managed to do it, despite me feeling like I was never going to be sober. But I am proud, so proud to say that I am now over eight years sober".

Now for most people breaking free from long term addiction would be wonderful and inspiring enough, but this is Gina, so get ready because there is more to come...

"Tackling that, which was so hard, meant I was then open to new opportunities and the Universe (as it always does if we are open to receive), gave me the keys to a golden future by showing me to a new work opportunity".

"I was looking for something I could do from home that was both ethical and environmentally friendly, I wanted financial freedom, and was fed up with bosses, especially male ones".

"Joining the company meant that I had the tools to tackle the weight problem I had literally been carrying around, I was a typical yo-yo dieter, and had struggled all my life. But I managed to step off that merry go round too and have been at my ideal weight and size for five years now. This is something that I had never achieved before".

So, here we now have a sober, slimmer Gina (and believe me she is almost unrecognisable, I have seen the photos!). But again, she was ready to push forward.

“I have always said how much the business has affected my personal development, one of the things I struggled with when I first started was my lack of confidence about driving. From home to the shops, or to work and back, what I called the golden triangle was ok, but ask me to step outside of my comfort zone and I was terrified".

"Then I had to go to my first ever company event at our head office in Warwick, I was so excited! I got on the motorway, feeling very smug and proud, only to realise *eventually* that I was going completely the wrong way!”

“And was on my way to Bristol, not Warwick! It was quite a long journey to be able to get on the right track, but I made it in the end”.

With her wealth of experience of triumphing over adversity Gina told me she works on the principle “if you want change in your life of any sort, then YOU have to make the decision to change. It is within our hands but is up to us to grasp opportunities and take steps and action to get us to where we want to go, to step into who we want to become".

And for Gina stepping out of her comfort zone is the only way to live.

EDEN

There are many experiences that I will not be including in this telling of my story, but hopefully there will be more than enough to inspire you.

I never fitted in, definitely not at school where everything was so noisy and boisterous, I did enjoy the learning, and many of my school reports showed me as doing well academically, but my absenteeism and lack of connection in class was always commented on.

At home mum was seriously mentally unwell and couldn't give us the care and attention that we needed. Other family members stepped in to fill the practical gaps where they could, but I always felt like I was floating emotionally, and even as a young child was very lonely.

By the time I was halfway through senior school I had overwhelming anxiety about going to school, and virtually anywhere else. Having full blown passing out panic attacks when I went out, or when my parents went out without me leaving me home alone.

I was seen by a professor at Great Ormond Street Hospital for some time, and his general thoughts were – if she wants to do something she will. Again, the message fed back to me was all around stop misbehaving, no-one tried to speak my language or really unravel the problem of why is this child struggling?

Even people who were aware how bad things were at home didn't reach out. This may have been the old idea that family business is private business, I will never really understand that mentality.

When I was at school I was a target for a certain group of bullies, and was taunted for my unusual behaviour caused by my sensitivity. My appearance, being smaller than everyone else, my lack of friends or doing well in class, you name it they found a way to taunt me for it.

Eventually school was over and I had actually managed to pass some exams. Although I wanted to get a job to earn my own money, and work on becoming independent, my mum had other ideas and after seeking advice from my uncle on what courses I should do, sent me to college. Where I actually made a couple of friends, ironically this caused me to struggle academically, as all I wanted to do was hang out with them. And I was asked to leave within three months.

My anxiety turned into full blown agoraphobia,

which kept me at home for the next few years, and as my family didn't have a computer I could use, it was incredibly isolating.

Eventually I worked with enough therapists across enough disciplines to start to build an identity for myself, tackling my phobia enough to start a very part time voluntary job.

Having a tricky relationship with my parents led to my being asked to leave home at twenty. With no social support and no money my options were extremely limited, and I had to turn to the local authority for help. At that time, I was too young to be given a tenancy of my own, and I was placed in a homelessness hostel.

It was fine during the day, but at night the older residents would bully the younger more vulnerable ones. So, I stopped using the shared facilities altogether, zapping meals in a microwave in my room, washing at the sink and peeing in a bucket.

Even then they would bang on the door shouting and trying to be intimidating - which they absolutely were.

Throughout the time I was there I tried to find paid work, but as soon as people saw where I lived, they wouldn't even meet me. Then I got wise and used my parents address, and got my first job in business development, with a new start up which I loved.

Luckily, it only took six months in the hostel before I

was old enough to have a tenancy and be allocated a flat. People gave me a cooker and fridge that they were replacing with new ones, and my then boyfriend's parents gave us a bed and television.

I was proud of my new flat and ready for a new start.

It was definitely different, but not what I had hoped for, as the next couple of years were stained by that same boyfriend's violence and abusive behaviour. I have no doubt had I not left he would have killed me (as he often said he would) in one of his tempers.

Like many women I left and went back on a few occasions, believing that it was somehow me, and that if I tried harder it would all be ok.

One day I confided in my boss about what was going on, and he helped me feel that I could survive if I left, even giving me a company car so that I could get about.

I can still see my ex partner standing in the window with his arms folded watching, on the day I left. He thought I would be back, but this time I was gone for good, all I took with me was the clothes I was wearing and a twenty pound note stolen from his wallet. At that time people's views on domestic abuse was somewhat different than it is now. If you didn't leave immediately the question was why? people didn't hold back about asking the victim what they had done to cause the violence.

That judgement sat festering away with all the other negative opinions I had been given about myself, and I internalised the blame for what had happened.

When I asked the housing officer to help me get him out of my flat his response was "you got him in there, you get him out". It wasn't going to be possible to live there safely, even if he did leave.

So, I made the choice to walk away from the flat and go to the bottom of the housing list.

The years went by, I rented rooms when I had work, or stayed with my parents, although that was never a healthy solution.

Overall, everything was heading in the right direction. I had rebuilt my life, had a career that included working in the marketing department of a traditional publishing house, which I loved and was managing my anxiety to a reasonable degree.

After eleven years I was offered another tenancy, and got my lovely flat, I didn't even care that it needed two industrial cleans, only had a sink in the kitchen, needed rewiring and had no heating, I knew it would be lovely.

Then I met someone and got married, it wasn't easy as he came into the relationship with debt, then he stopped working, met someone else and left. After he was gone I found he had run up huge debts in our joint names.

Just as I was processing that blow, I was made redundant. My belongings were repossessed around me, and I was terrified that my home would be one of the things that I lost again.

It seemed like I was going back in time and losing everything that I had worked for. I was so scared that this would break me, it was like I was losing my sanity this time.

The anxiety came back with full force, but rather than panic attacks or racing thoughts, it was pure terror. I would just need to escape the pain and disconnect.

The physical symptoms would last for hours, and I stopped doing everything. I wasn't well enough to live on my own full time, and no-one could stay with me, so that meant going back to my parents as there was no-one else in my life.

It was an intensely lonely period, I never met anyone like me, and the professionals I met treated me as if I could just stop my symptoms if I tried hard enough.

One day I was listening to a piece on Radio Four about disability, and they mentioned Personal Budgets. These had been created to enable people with long term conditions or disabilities to live an independent life (whatever that might look like for them).

I asked my psychiatrist at my quarterly appointment about it, he said he had never heard of them and sent me away. I did my research and found out that they really did exist, so the next appointment I asked again, and was fobbed off.

He said social services might deal with it, and I needed to tell my social worker, but I didn't have one! So, I referred myself to the department, explained the issues and the person I spoke to told me what to say to my psychiatrist.

At my next appointment I challenged him saying "I know that it is you who signs off on the budgets!" and laughing he agreed to start the paperwork. Eventually, after assessments and a mountain of paperwork I was awarded enough funds to pay for a support worker three hours a week.
Three hours where I could do what I wanted, go out for a coffee, go to a shop. Also, importantly this gave me a chance to go into private therapy, as I could now get to sessions.

This therapist helped me sort many of the things I had carried with me, and suggested that I may have a trauma condition rather than anxiety. The more I read about that, the more it seemed to fit.

We continued like this with my three hours a week for some time until my parents wanted to move away. After many emails, letters, calls, meetings and the intervention of an advocate my award was increased to sixty hours.

Luckily they didn't end up moving as I don't know what would have happened for the other hundred plus hours of the week.

But this was fabulous, I now had the chance to lead something much closer to the life that I wanted to have. And I bravely signed up for a six week creative course for women, that my support worker would accompany me to.

One of those weeks we were asked if courage was in abundant supply what we would do, and without a thought I said that I would be a writer.
That thought stayed with me over the following months, and at the beginning of the next year I set up a free website and started blogging my stories.

They were being read around the world and were well received, in fact people said that I was funny and should write a sitcom or a book. It seemed like a book would be easier, so that's what I did.

It was the year after my first book was published that I was given a diagnosis of Complex Post Traumatic Stress Disorder. Apparently, it hadn't been possible to say this before as it wasn't recognised in the official diagnostic manual. So even though the NHS specialists knew I had the condition they couldn't write it in my notes.

As I write this I now have four humour collections, and five non fiction books across three pen names, and have gone on to become one of a handful of Alliance of Independent Authors approved publishing consultants mentoring writers globally.

Through social media I found out there is a lot of cross over between neurodiversity and Complex PTSD, and when one of my favourite content creators took the RAADS autism questionnaire, I did too and scored 165 out of 200.

I decided that score needed further investigating, and after researching an organisation that would be recognised by the NHS and social services used my savings to book a private assessment.

After multiple questionnaires filled out by me, my dad and a long term friend. A full day of testing and interviews I was finally given the missing piece of the puzzle - my ADHD Autism diagnosis aged fifty.

There was a couple of weeks of disbelief, that no-one had ever really seen me, and anger that I could have had the right support had they known.

That didn't last long, and I allowed my love of research to take over as I just tried to learn as much about myself and what my diagnosis meant for me.

Two years down the line I accept myself as an AuDHD person with a spiky profile and lots of sensory issues. My days seem more manageable, as I know that my anxiety, wobbles, inability to do things or mood changes, will likely be coming from too much noise, lights, or information – or all of these things at once.

There are some new autistic friends who accept me as I am, and me them. There have been people who don't believe I am autistic, but as they aren't trained professionals and usually have little actual knowledge of what autism really means, I don't waste my energy arguing, and leave them to their opinions.

I am so thankful to have discovered that I was never failing at life, I just didn't have the right information to be my best self, and now I do.

Like everyone else I do not know what life holds for me. And I don't make predictions in regard to my CPTSD and how much my levels of independence might change.

Being a published author had been a long term dream of mine, and now not only have I achieved that, but I have also been able to start helping others. It is something I am immensely proud of, no, it doesn't change my being disabled, but it does change how I see my potential.

I have survived so much, that many day to day things that might bother others just don't register with me. I refuse to be broken.

RESOURCES

UK
British Association for Counselling and Psychotherapy
https://www.bacp.co.uk/
The Samaritans:
https://www.samaritans.org/
Mind:
https://www.mind.org.uk/
Citizens advice:
https://www.citizensadvice.org.uk/
Financial:
https://www.moneyhelper.org.uk/en

Claire's law
The right to know if your partner has an abusive past. Also known as the Domestic Violence Disclosure Scheme (DVDS) is a police policy giving people the right to know if their current or ex-partner has any previous history of violence or abuse.

Under Clare's Law, you have the right to:

Make an application to the police requesting information about your current or ex-partner, because you are worried they may have been abusive in the past and believe they may pose a risk to you in future.

Request information from the police about the current or ex-partner of a close friend, neighbour or family member, because you are concerned that they might be at risk of domestic abuse in future.

This is called the 'right to ask.' You have a right to ask the police no matter if your enquiry relates to a heterosexual or same-sex relationship, as long as you are aged 16 or older. You also have the right to ask about a partner regardless of your (or your neighbour, friend or family member's) gender identity, ethnicity, race, religion or other characteristics.

You also have the 'right to know'. This means that if police checks show that your current or ex-partner has a record of violent or abusive behaviour, and they believe you may be at risk, they may decide to proactively share that information with you. If you're worried that your current or former partner has been abusive or violent in the past, Clare's Law was created to formally give you the right to find out.
https://www.clares-law.com/

USA
American Counselling Association:
https://www.counseling.org/

Free legal advice
https://www.americanbar.org/groups/legal_services/flh-home/flh-free-legal-help/
Suicide & Crisis Lifeline: Call 988 for immediate support
Financial support
https://www.nonprofitpoint.com/free-financial-assistance-organizations/

State-Level Domestic Violence Laws: Many states have laws addressing domestic violence. These laws often include provisions for restraining orders, protective orders, and mandatory reporting requirements.
Background Checks: While not specifically designed for domestic violence disclosure, background checks can reveal criminal records, including past convictions for violent offenses.
Megan's Law and Sex Offender Registries: All 50 states have Megan's Law legislation that requires sex offenders to register with state authorities. This information is often publicly available, allowing communities to be informed about the presence of registered sex offenders.
Duty to Warn Laws: Some states have "duty to warn" laws, requiring mental health professionals to warn potential victims if a patient has made credible threats of violence.

Canada

Canadian professional counsellor association
https://www.thecpca.ca/
Mental Health Support:
https://www.canada.ca/en/public-health/services/mental-health-services/mental-health-get-help.html
Financial Support:
https://www.canada.ca/en/services/benefits/benefits-financial-support.html
Clare's Law
https://www.pathssk.org/clares-law/

Australia
Australian Counselling Association:
https://www.theaca.net.au/home
Australian helplines and hotlines
https://www.findahelpline.com/countries/au
Mental Health Support:
https://www.healthdirect.gov.au/mental-health-helplines
Financial support:
https://www.moneysmart.gov.au/financial-advice
Debt Advice:
https://www.ndh.org.au/financial-counselling/find-a-financial-counsellor/
Northern Territories:
https://www.nt.gov.au/law/crime/domestic-family-and-sexual-violence
Western Australia:
https://www.wa.gov.au/government/family-and-domestic-violence

South Australia
https://www.police.sa.gov.au/your-safety/dvds

How to Connect With The Inspirational Women

Yvonne
https://www.linkedin.com/in/yvonne-mark-b212aa3b/

Cassie
https://www.edengruger.com/edens-articles-and-interviews

Kelly
https://www.kellygatescoaching.com

Kate
https://www.squigglyink.com

Monica
http://www.educarefund.org.uk/

Lesley
https://www.tottielimejuice.com

Kanan
https://www.kanancoaching.com/

Nari
https://www.ajvirlf.com

Moriah
https://www.moriahjane.com/

Anita

https://www.ad-accounting.co.uk

Teresa
https://www.dukesconsultancy.co.uk/

Sam
https://www.wiseheartsam.com

Elizabeth
https://www.elizabeth-grand.com/

Ruth
https://www.wibn.co.uk

Jacqueline
https://www.wegrantfitnessandhealth.co.uk

Sarah
https://www.ticboxproductions.co.uk

Becs
https://www.becsbradley.com

Gina
https://www.facebook.com/georginaannmann

Eden
https://www.edengruger.com

Please do leave a review for this book from wherever you bought it, to help other people find their way to it.

https://www.amazon.ca/Strength-Survival-Stories-Sian-West-ebook/dp/B0GM8Y6FGN

Scroll down to below the book details and you'll see a button to leave a review

https://www.edengruger.com/sian-west

www.ingramcontent.com/pod-product-compliance
Lightning Source LLC
La Vergne TN
LVHW010627100826
845148LV00014B/3141

9781738524853